The Cheetah

Fast as Lightning

Text by Philippe Dupont
and Valérie Tracqui

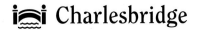 Charlesbridge

In this heat, nothing is better than a good nap!

Always worried, the graceful impalas think they heard a noise . . . . Could the cheetah be near?

4

Far, far away, in Africa...

At noon, the heat is overwhelming. The African grasslands, green from all the rain, stretch as far as the eye can see. Herds of gazelle graze peacefully, while zebra and antelope doze in the shade of the trees. The steady buzzing of insects is the only sound that breaks the silence.

Not far away lies a cheetah, hidden in the tall grass. It too is resting.

For wildcats, a yawn is more a sign of hunger than of sleepiness! What big teeth!

Four cubs means a lot of work!

By late afternoon it begins to cool down, and the cheetahs become active again. The impalas don't have to worry yet because the female cheetah is busy with her babies. Three months after mating, she gave birth to four adorable cubs. She must raise them on her own. What a lot of work!

The male and female cheetah are together only during mating. Then the male leaves the female — the cubs will never know their father.

Baby cheetahs spend their early days sleeping or feeding on their mother's rich milk.

Other types of big cats share the work of caring for their babies. A male leopard will bring meat to the female. Male and female lions watch over their young. But the mother cheetah must take care of her cubs all by herself. Every day she finds a new spot in the tall grasses where she can hide the cubs while she goes off to hunt. The newborn cubs are completely helpless.

One by one, the mother carries her cubs in her mouth by the fur of the neck.

The cubs' eyes have not yet opened, and they weigh only 10 ounces — no more than a small grapefruit.

Yumm!
A tasty meal

A brown hare rushes through the bushes. It hears a sound and turns its head — too late. The hungry mother cheetah doesn't miss this chance for a meal. In a couple of leaps, she seizes the hare by the neck and kills it. Then she hurries back to eat it near her cubs.

This hare is just the right size to make a good meal for the mother.

In order to make milk for her cubs, the mother needs to eat well. She has to hunt every day. Otherwise, she would be happy eating just once every two or three days.

The cheetah can last ten days without water. It's a good thing, because water isn't always nearby.

8

This curious cub didn't miss a thing.

Never let them out of sight!

The days go by. The cheetah cubs are now six weeks old and very playful. Sometimes the mother makes them behave with a swat of her paw. Usually, however, she very patiently lets them do as they like, and licks them tenderly.

Most importantly, she never lets them out of her sight. She knows that the jackal is not far away and that if she loses sight of her babies, he might attack them.

Motionless, the jackal waits for its chance.

The cubs drink their mother's milk until they are two or three months old, but they begin learning to eat meat at the age of six weeks.

You must eat meat, little one, if you want to grow up big like your mom. She weighs 88 pounds — ten times more than you!

Fortunately, the thick silver mane covering a baby cheetah's back and head helps it blend in perfectly with the savannah grasses. This mane will protect a cub until it is two and a half months old.

The mother cheetah gives a gentle little lick to show her affection. Everything is fine.

Baby cheetahs can climb trees using their sharp claws. By the time they are six months old their claws will be worn down and useless for climbing.

Ready, jump! To be a good hunter, you must be very light on your feet.

"Stay right here, I'm going off to hunt."

Learn to hunt by playing

Now four months old, the lively, young cheetahs need to get ready for their future lives as hunters.

The cubs constantly chase and catch each other — they tumble about, and snap at each other. They take turns at playing the hunter and the prey. This play is all for fun.

Right now the cubs are playing, but soon these skills will be a matter of life and death.

Hunting is an art

The mother spots a herd of peacefully grazing gazelles. She concentrates on one of them who has strayed a bit away from the group. She crouches down, stretches her neck forward, and very, very slowly creeps toward the gazelle. Her golden fur blends in with the dry yellow grasses so that she is very hard to see.

The cubs obey their mother by staying together and not moving from the spot where she left them. But they don't miss a bit of the hunt. They learn by watching.

A cheetah may spend several hours sneeking up on its prey. What patience!

These Thomson's gazelles are not aware of any danger. At the slightest danger, though, they will dash off at full speed.

This gazelle has wandered off away from the others.

Suddenly the gazelles look up! Did they see something? Instantly, the cheetah stops moving. Seeing nothing, the gazelles begin to graze again, and the mother cheetah again creeps toward them. She slinks through the long grasses, slips behind a little mound, and finally crouches behind a bush.

Luckily, the wind hasn't carried the cheetah's scent to the gazelle. That's a good thing because two out of three times the cheetah fails to catch her prey. This time, she is close enough to capture it.

The cheetah is the fastest mammal in the world, reaching an incredible 62 miles per hour at top speed. It runs out of breath quickly, however, and cannot keep up this pace for a long time.

Fast as lightning

The cheetah comes out of hiding about 160 feet away from the gazelle. She starts off at a trot. By the time the herd has realized its danger, the cheetah is less than a hundred feet away. As the gazelles spread out, the cheetah speeds up.

Her run becomes a series of great big leaps. She almost seems to be flying. As she gets closer, the gazelle zigzags sharply, trying to lose its attacker. But the cheetah twists and turns using her long tail to keep her balance as she changes direction.

This is it! With one hit of her paw, the cheetah knocks the gazelle down, and the hunt is over.

A cheetah's jaws are not powerful enough to inflict a fatal bite, so it must strangle its prey by biting its neck in exactly the right place. It's difficult but effective.

Time to eat

As soon as possible, the mother cheetah signals her hungry cubs to join her. They have watched from a distance, and they respond at once to her sharp little call. The cubs immediately start eating, but their exhausted mother lies panting for fifteen minutes.

Then she begins to eat. There's no time to lose. Other meat-eating animals will soon arrive.

When her cubs were still young, the cheetah could feed them on rabbits and young gazelles, which were easy to catch. Now her babies need bigger prey.

"Let's have a bite of this animal while Mom catches her breath. Isn't it tough!"

An adult cheetah can eat almost 6 1/2 pounds of fresh meat every day. What is left over is eaten by the other meat-eaters of the savannah.

Attracted by the scent, the hyena approaches. The cheetahs have hardly finished eating when they must give up their food to this powerful predator. Soon jackals and vultures will be in charge of picking the carcass clean.

After the cheetah has done all the hard work, hyenas, lions, and sometimes even leopards will come to steal the food.

All four cubs are still alive. Often, two out of three die from sickness or are killed by another animal.

Family life

The well-fed cubs grow up quickly. They now have a proud look in their eyes. But they still have to stay together as a family for many months until they are able to hunt for themselves.

Each family has its own territory, or area in which it hunts. It takes skill to defend this territory. Usually cheetahs move to new areas as they follow the wandering herds that are their prey.

Once they are grown up, these young males will fight over territory. They will mark the borders of their territory with scratches on the bark of trees, and by leaving their scent.

This young cheetah, showing his teeth, is not smiling. The goal of these snarls and battles between brothers and sisters is to learn how to act when they are out in the world with no family to protect them.

Leaving home

The young cheetahs have been practicing their hunting methods for many months. They have lost their silver manes, and the time for playing is over. Their practice fights look ferocious. The cheetahs bite at each other's necks and roll around in the dust. But they know when to stop before anyone gets hurt.

One day, it will be mating season once more, and the mother cheetah will go off with a male cheetah, leaving her nearly full-grown babies to fend for themselves.

This is the big day. The young cheetahs are now a year and a half old, and their family life is over. While the two brothers join a band of bachelor males, their sisters will live alone.

No rest for the cheetah

The cheetah's future is threatened. This cat has many natural enemies that are more powerful. Even in the national parks, where it is a protected species, tourists come and disturb it. What can be done to save this champion runner?

Thoughtless tourists come so close that there's no way the cheetah can hunt!

The competition

The cheetah is not strong enough to prevent other animals from stealing the prey that it has killed. Little by little, lions force it to live in areas that are too hilly or too open. The cheetah's hunting techniques do not work well in these types of areas.

The nervous cheetah finds it hard to eat its fill, because even a flock of vultures can frighten it off.

The tourists

For thousands of years, people used cheetahs to help them hunt. Now the cheetah is almost extinct in Asia, and it has become extremely rare in Africa. Even in the national parks the cheetah cannot hunt in peace. Cars frighten away prey, and tourists taking pictures spoil a great number of chases.

To learn more about the cheetah's way of life, scientists have fitted a radio collar around this cheetah's neck. They can tell where it goes by listening to the beeps on their radio receiver.

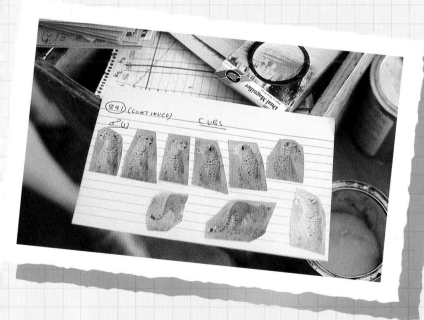

Each individual cheetah has its own file. In order to tell the cheetahs apart, the scientists record individual markings such as the number of black rings along the tail, or marks behind the ears.

Protection

Scientists in Tanzania are studying cheetah behavior so that people can protect them. A starving cheetah will sometimes kill farm animals, which naturally makes it unpopular with farmers. The protectors of the cheetah are trying to make local people value cheetahs. The future of this splendid creature depends upon the creation of special areas where other meat-eating animals and tourism can be controlled and limited.

The spotted cat family

The cheetah, the leopard, the jaguar, the serval, and the ocelot are all members of the spotted cat family. Like the house cat, they are very good hunters. Quick and flexible, they can move silently. Their graceful bodies and beautiful markings help them blend into their surroundings. What else do these big cats have in common? All face the threat of extinction because they are hunted for their fur.

Let's look at each one.

The *leopard,* or *panther*, has ring-shaped spots and beautiful green eyes. Its legs are shorter than a cheetah's, and its body is heavier. It climbs trees very well and likes to rest and eat its prey there. It mostly hunts at night, lying in wait and pouncing on its prey.

The *serval,* a much smaller cat, can be recognized by its large ears and short tail. It has long legs, and its spots form a pattern of stripes. In some areas of Africa, there are servals with no spots at all. It weighs between 13 and 33 pounds, which is very light compared to the jaguar which weighs between 132 and 253 pounds.

The *jaguar* looks a lot like the leopard, but it is larger. Its head and paws are much bigger. Its ring-shaped spots are also bigger. The most obvious difference, however, is that the leopard and the cheetah live in Africa and Asia, while the jaguar lives only in the jungles of Central and South America.

The *ocelot* is the smallest spotted cat. Its fur has markings of many shapes and sizes. It is a good swimmer and an excellent climber. The ocelot chases small prey among the branches of trees, and like the jaguar, it lives in the forests of Central and South America. What a magnificent family!

For Further Reading on Cheetahs . . .

Esbensen, Barbara. <u>Swift as the Wind: The Cheetah</u>. Orchard, 1995.

MacMillan, Diane. <u>Cheetahs.</u> Carolrhoda, 1998.

Morrison, Taylor. <u>Cheetah.</u> Holt, 1998.

Thompson, Sharon Elaine. <u>Built for Speed: The Extraordinary, Enigmatic Cheetah.</u> Lerner, 1998.

To See Cheetahs in Captivity . . .

Folzenlogen, Darcy and Robert. <u>The Guide to American Zoos and Aquariums</u>. Willow Press, 1993.

Many zoos also have web sites on the internet. To learn more about their exhibits, go to the following page on the Yahoo WWW site:

http://dir.yahoo.com/Science/Biology/Zoology/Zoos

Use the Internet to Find Out More about Cheetahs . . .

Cheetah Conservation Fund
—Find out how the cheetah got its spots and other amazing information. See many photographs and participate in an adoption program. Includes coloring book pages.
    http://cheetah.org

Cheetah Survival Home Page
—See fast facts and more detailed information about the life of a cheetah.
    http://www.emunix.emich.edu/~fitspatr/cheetah/cheetah.html

The Cheetah Spot
—Hear a cheetah chirping, see safari photos, and find more references and links.
    http://www.cheetahspot.com

Discovery Online: Cheetah Cam
—See the cheetah enclosure at the Oklahoma Zoo and learn about the Species Survival Plan.
    http://www.discovery.com/cams/cheetah/cheetahmain.html

See Updated Animal Close-Ups Internet Resources . . .
    http://www.charlesbridge.com

Photograph credits

JACANA: Arthus Bertrand p. 6 (bottom), p.7 (bottom), p. 10 (bottom), p. 11, p. 12, p. 14 (top), p. 15 (top), p. 18, p. 19 (top), p. 22, p. 24-25 (center), Varin, Visage p. 23 (top); Denis-Huot: p. 6 (top), p. 23 (bottom), Degré: p. 9, Cordier p. 26 (bottom), Robert p. 8, Gohier p. 27 (bottom).
GUERRIER: p. 10 (top), p. 13 (top), p. 14 (bottom), p. 24 (bottom).
TRACQUI: p. 15 (bottom).
GUENOT: p. 19 (bottom).
DENIS-HOUT: p. 25 (top right, bottom left).
ZIESLER: p. 3, p. 4-5 (background), p. 16 (top left and background), p. 13 (bottom), p. 5 (right).
NATURE: Polking: p. 4 (top), p. 17 (bottom right), p. 20-21; Gohier p. 27 (top).
DARMON: p. 26 (top).